A Black Odyssey

A Black Odyssey: collected poems
Copyright ©2012 SETH

ISBN: 978-0-9882279-2-7
Publisher: Mercury HeartLink
Albuquerque, New Mexico
Printed in the United States of America

Back cover and interior photographs of SETH
by Kit Hedman, www.hedmanphoto.com

Front cover serigraph "Odysseus" (detail)
by Rein Whitt-Pritchette. (see p. 115)

Contact: seth@wagingart.com

Mercury HeartLink
www.heartlink.com

A Black **Odyssey**

collected poems

SETH

Contents

ACKNOWLEDGMENTS

I have a reputation for taking risks. Truth is, I just don't know any better. Ostensibly, this collection is my attempt to cram 30 years of poetry into one volume. Not wishing to publish them in chronological order, group them according to time period or by style and content, I opted to arrange them according to my favorite epic tale. Why not? Odysseus is my favorite literary hero. Many of my poems reference some aspect of his journey. Plus, his trials and triumphs have often served as a beacon to several of my own struggles, lighting a clear path during periods of uncertainty.

No matter how I arranged these poems, I could not justify getting all my poetry included. Considerations of pacing, theme and tone required I leave a few favored poems out. Nevertheless I managed to squeeze in a good ninety-eight percent of what I regard as my best poetry. The reader will find early poems mixed with more mature ones – different styles intermingling as if they were distant cousins whose only similarity is their sprouting from the same family tree...and that together they narrate a cohesive story.

As with any of my more ambitious undertakings, this volume took years to bring to fruition. I have far too many people to thank than I can possibly remember. My apologies to all those I neglect to mention.

First and foremost, there is Stewart S. Warren without whose support, guidance and gentle wisdom this volume would not be possible. I am also indebted to Linda Giedl, one of the earliest champions of this ambitious idea. For proofreading I have Roseanna Frechette, Sally Ortiz and Charles Nichols to thank – each of whom graciously agreed to navigate my sometimes rocky, often unconventional use of literary devices.

I wish also to pay tribute to my many muses, each a goddess in her own right: Melinda Mlinac, Pamela Cashdollar, Becky Snyder, Denise Darinsig, Stephanie Selene Anderson, Shawn Edwards & Sandra Alikky Hernandez. Without their grace, sisterly affection and warm acceptance this at times shaky vessel might have capsized years ago. Special mention goes out to Mary Kinsey to whom I dedicate the chapter *Isle of Ogygia*.

I wish also to send an *Ahoy Mateys* to my sundry crewmates, fellow sailors and partners in rhyme, beginning with Tupper Cullum and Woody Hildebrant, Roseanna Frechette and Alton Ghrist...and extending to everyone who has ever performed with Open Rangers. Likewise to all former and current members of Art Compost & the Word Mechanics, all of whom enabled me to fine tune and add the much needed finishing polish to many of the poems contained within. Among this motley crew I also add my colleagues from Jafrika, Ricki Harada and Chris Macor, our voyage among the most rewarding of my career. And lest I forget, I send a shout out to two additional shipmates, Judah Freed and Lenny Chernila, both first mates of the highest caliber.

Finally I owe a tremendous debt to all the various open mic venues and stages Denver and the Rocky Mountain Region have opened to me – and to all the ears who have listened to earlier versions of the poetry contained herewithin. I am especially grateful to Julie Cummings and Ziggies Live Music Bar for allowing me to test drive this volume chapter by chapter before a live gathering, to Barb Test who deserves the appellation "saint" and to the Columbine Poets who have always had my back. I will be forever grateful to Joe D'Rose and his Muddy's Java Café and doubly so to Marilyn Megenity for her many many many years of support, as well as to her magical Mercury Café which continues to this day to nurture the vital organs of my poetic spirit.

May the Word continue to be with them all.

—SETH

PREFACE

Life is a voyage...and I am a man, a mere mortal. Like Homer's Odysseus, I have chosen to navigate life's oceans and climb her peaks relying mainly on my wit, my guile, my intellect. Athena has favored us both. Apollo has also shined a few rays my way. Like Odysseus, I have had to outwit the Cyclops, deflect Circe's charms, circumnavigate the sweet songs of the sirens. I too have traversed the underworld, basked on the island of the sun-god and allowed Calypso to salve my wounds. Eventually, I found a way home. And like Odysseus & the Everyman in Milton's *Paradise Regained*, managed to reclaim a kingdom that was always already mine.

This, then, is my journey.....

for Colette,
my Penelope

A Poet Petitions his Muse

Every day it's that blank page
a smooth flat placid white man
                          of a face
glowering up at me
        eyes narrowed, mouth clamped shut
        black dash   thin as an eyelash

Two teaspoon of tears
        half a cup of memory
        marinate in disappointment's chair
Soon similes smear on lipstick
        collide into commas & colons
                          calling itself Poetry

"Forever. . .is a long time," she says
        straightening her skirt
                crevice crinkling her forehead

The threadbare down brewskis
Con men don themselves in comedy
The dying contemplate skinny waitresses
        Reluctantly I enter
        this land of the bleeding
where the discontent set fire
                to paper sticks
conducting wholy mass
        over sauerkraut & mustard

"Let it bleed," the next poet says
"Open your window; God is rain."

● ● ●

There are rivers damned in me
silver wet knives
       Love   Hate   Pain   Envy
       splash & dribble
       roar & rumble   grumble like a storm
with nowhere to pour free

There is a mountain staid in me
cragged, jagged, lonely   icicle tears
       trickling
       into streams
that tumble   becoming the rivers
       damned
       in me

There are cities lost in me
shards of shattered decomposed history   marbled halls
       where dark purple-clad warriors
       once fondled Cleopatra's knee
laughing in the naked darkness
sighing as they measure
       the infinite stars
while weathering the raging sea

Tho gone be the elephanted armies
           their hoofbeats pound on still
           in hymn and horn
           and pencil.

•••

If I could rub this midnight lamp
          and win three wishes for my words
The first I'd wish is for thy Will
          to pump my heart and through my pen
Thy Wisdom spill, for sentences
          like circling birds: to be your stamp

Is my prime wish, to wrestle true
          through mud and mire, not like the priest
Who idols books, but as a soiled
          prophet, a wrestler of tigers,
A Samson wielding syllables
          that name the beast, sweep clear the view

That ripple like rivers, that sigh.
          As to a second wish – I'd wish
Upon each page your flow and Grace;
          that from my pen in Beauty's skirt
Your sway, your swish, your pining winds
          might pierce the age, your tall oaks cry.

In such Beauty, serene, sublime,
          that ruffles waves and whitens clouds
Dip my ink, mirror creation,
          my paragraphs please harmonize
With eagles proud, give wings to my
          imagination; yours make mine.

Then, should I hazard one last wish:
      to nouns and verbs and adjectives
I'd wish for Love's pure consonants,
      for vowels round as wedding rings,
For marriage 'twixt sound and substance
      in form caressed, creator kissed.

Or does this wish them all embrace?
      Perhaps a pen in love with words
With content wrapped in lover's vows
      need not invoke your confidence;
Perhaps in Love my words right placed
      will win your Will, your Love, your Grace.

TELEMACHUS

A pimply-chinned black boy
Nose running, sneaker untied,
His dirty oval face, a brown egg
With two dark saucer eyes
His undernourished body
Dwarfed by the gap in the teeth
Of the woman at his side –
Her brusque commands, her angry replies
To his curious questions
So he hums, sings, talks to himself
While lost youth seethes in her breast
like an exhausted tide.

Rattled in the mass transit vehicle
Two distant travelers abide
She destined for nowhere, he
Settling back for the long lonely ride.

●●●

Pain be my mother
no gentle mistress she
who weaned me on the milk of misery
onto a son of man

Babe in swaddling clothes
mourning's mellow son
writhing in linen torn under shadows spun
in webs of reprimand

Madonna a shrew
pawn of Aeolus' wind;
heartache my savior; a son of sin
soaked to its weeping crest

Where Hopelessness pitied,
Grief wept and Affliction flew
with alms of Patience and Endurance
who spoke of the curséd being blessed:

"Hurt is the lesson:
the sage's cutting stone;
the force behind ocean's woeful clashing moan
where martyrs' bones walk calm

Pain is a mentor:
Love's lieutenant – a shield of scars
aligning taut limits that bid men
yield to tear's persuasive psalms

Eternity is forever testing;
no skin escapes its mark
to listen is to learn, to run to embark
on Tragedy's Row for

False is the desire
that disparages to earn
each moment, for Challenge is your true sojourn:
let discovery overflow."

• • •

My name is Immanuel. I have a mission.
My name is Ezekial. My name is Ezra. My name
is Marcus, Jesus, Jude. My name is the same
as dour-faced sibyl, cheek-boned, virginal,
ear-pressed soul-poised for the thunder-throbbing
lightning bolt of Zeus. My name is Lao. My name is
Benedict, Tomas, Baruch, Leonardo. I am
the smile of Mona Lisa, the swagger
of David, the hand-clutched 30 pieces of silver
on a wall in Milan. My name is Nathaniel,
Fyodor, Hermann. My name is Joan. My name:
the same as countless bearded skeletons
whose bony fingers traced the covenant,
the desert my podium; I am wind
scalding sand, reciting tales of oceans
and floods. My name is Leo.
My name is Miguel. My name is Jacque.
Men call me fool.

2

Born of woman's wound
   a seed plopped in passion
        cropped in passivity;
   a deed dropped in plastics
        toppled by shame & pilfering poverty;

Our father who art in heaven –
                    hollowed be His name
   cracking his whip, strapping the snapping reins
to those cloud-thundering steeds,
Poseidon's sea-weeded trident
        wedged between powerful knees,
                stretching the four ocean-rollicking

corners to this porpoise-tumbling
fish-glistening green slimy sea

My father: ruling with five hands on every finger.

3

A babe   in a mangy manger
turtlenecked crew-cut red-necked wisemen
bearing boxed monoxide in crisp colorful packaging
(ribboned & bowed with the taut sinews
    of finely lynched Negroes)
Frankenstein and quagmire adorn my feet
Golden arches crack the privately-funded darkness
Christ masses an Inquisition –
        boosting the sale of torture racks
    (Government makes a killing in taxes)
Excalibur now calibrated into flab;
cardiacs get arrested; craniums get arthritis;
A babe   in a mangy manger
with a modest beard... and a mission.

4

Oh foolish imbecilic mission–
to revise wrung-out romanticisms,
to raise mass-mutilated Lazarus,
to hand shake da Vinci,
thought-wrestle Socrates,
pin human limits to the mat
                for one eternal second.

5

Thus spake Zarathustra's shadow:
Excel, Exceed, Excellence. For there is glory still in your
child-molested race; you who are builders, inventors, creators,
connivers: for always impatient with Life's will that ye grow through
discomfort. Just as a tree has soul, flowers expression, chestnuts
personality so too your buildings, your test-tubes, your tragedies. Only
abandon ye not aesthetics: for Truth's neon glows inside Beauty, the
will to do well, to package each gesture in grace and style
as in obeisance to that greatest of beards, She-he-it
who birth forth Nature. A Tannhauser taut in tumbling strands
shall ye swim 'gainst straining tides, soaked and self-pitied,
until heralded atop that wet wave triumphant; so shall your story be
told. Seek excellence; the world doth follow.
Thus spat the snow-ladened shadow of Zarathustra.

6

I weep the departed Zarathustra. I weep the war never won
under a parrot gods say would slay his own son. Yet I harken
to the battle call, the trumpet's screech, the drums
beating no more rapidly than my thundering temples, my sword
sheathed in my soul and thru my every act
unholstered. I harken to the heels of Achilles, to the call
of Ulysses who never surrendered to less. I tempt
the tongue-lashing ocean; the roar of heedless, incessant
motion; the rocky calcified walls of failure.
Failure, my saliva flies to you on wingéd courage. My pride is blind
and nose not your odor. I have a mission
you can not cease. My name is Ulysses. My name is Daniel.
My name is SETH. Flesh withers but beware
this chisel: for should this ink slice true
all the world shall know your Big Bluff and men in new ages
shall make minced mockery of you.

7

But how? How to hold such heroic posturing
when gnawed and nibbled by the mice of Prof. Jones' clock?
How to wield so weighted an invisible sword
when one hand must replenish the pocket
the other stifle a yawn. No more the hero couched
on muscle-pounding sweat-shiny stallion; the pavement palpitates
under rubber hooves and metallic phallics. Routine
and rabid Reason are the statues in the square
(pelted by the pigeon doo of profits). It is
John Jr. the III who negotiates our contracts.
And yes, I too wrestle the urge to merge, to
deepen with one mate (as you say), to steady the waters, to stabilize,
string popcorn 'round young children-gathered christmas trees;
to share the love I now horde for these sentences.

But longing be magnet to objects desired; feelings
first frighten, to awaken, then enlighten.
I too hear the tick-tock of Time's shifting purpose
as I scour this ocean's depth in search of your weave.
But know ye this: my name is Immanuel. And I have a mission.

POLYPHEMUS

What do you do when the eyes lie
When common decency is strung out on morphine
And children dangle from limbs that bleed
Blood oozing like money down the gutter of their dreams?

What do you do when eyes are held hostage
When juries deliberate over forks and spoons
In kitchens you have only known by going down on your knees
When babies are feast for flies
And hopelessness becomes another man's meat?

What do you do when the I's lie
When the suits that once rebelled over the tax on tea
Refuse to walk with the dog that is their darker selves
And instead toss bones at rumors of its humanity?

What do you do when I's wax blind
When prostitutes and killers outstrip the weeds
When the obvious is slapped in jails
Raped from behind, let out on good behavior
After learning to mimic proper legal ease?

What do you do when the ayes lie
When fear conspires to drug the truth
When law becomes its lackey
And hatred does a few Hail Marys
Before returning to patrol the streets?

And what do you do when the babies cry
When brains pound the pavement
And drive-by shootings offer your Einsteins their only relief?

What do you do when the ayes lie?

• • •

I saw a black man blow his heart out
He was on stage where everyone could see
He wore a brass albatross around his neck
                        and spoke in tongues

All around pretty people chattered about hairdos
And last night's escapades
While the waitress brought drinks
                        and restrooms overflowed

All the while the black man bled
In colors no rainbow ever boasted
He spewed his guts across the room

Nobody noticed.

• • •

There is something
his smile
        can not see
    the fork of his influence can't
                hear the cries of beef
    no matter how high he climbs the wails
        of his ancestral tree

The (does she or doesn't she) blonde
        nurtures his seed
    her daily forgiveness conflicted
            bludgeoned
    in the sunbathing lap
            of disquieting luxury

She chides gently, obliquely. . .

For make no mistake
        he wields the bigger bat
                from his once queer shoulder

Flies disburse
        as he laps the honey,
        his M16 poised in case
                the worker bees
    demand more nectar
        in lieu of their
                broken backs

His son attends Harvard
    majors in humor & the
whip of quips that proclaim him
        a chip off the same
shoulder, off the same
            smile that can not see
the homeless panhandler
        that can not see
the child older than its mother
        that can not see
the awkward tongue
writhing under his boot heel
        or
the lamb lie down with the fag

that can not see
the martyrs or their bloodstains
or
innocence reamed in the headlights
of his god of free speech
that can not see
those split infinitives plotting
their revenge in the minor leagues
or
his own humanity nailed to the
cross of the dirty little
slut whose mother does his laundry
that can not see
those indians now called arabs
the ones with no inalienable rights
save to roll over, play dead
and look menacing
in his goliath tv screens
as he reaches for another beer
and cracks open another
smile that can not see.

● ● ●

There is no such person as the devil
he insisted
as flames flared from his eye sockets
and licked his face
like a black widow must lick
the lover she seduces   then fucks
before devouring.

It is stupor-stition,
                he ranted on
      clicking his cloven heels   for emphasis
          nervously twitching
                   his tail.

Man is in control of the planet
      And science and reason are king.

                 With that
    he turned back to his vials
        and test tubes
    and mixed   a molecule cocktail

      and somewhere far away   visible
    only on radar   and tv screens   subject to
       instant replay   and statistical analysis

    thousands went up in flames
      and the wail of orphans roared
                  like a furnace.

Like I said, he turned and winked at me
              adjusting his cap
    to accommodate his horns   of plenty
      there's no such thing as the devil,
there is only them
        and Me.

QUEEN OF AEAEA

Moon slips beneath silken sheets
Dolphins abandon shallow water
Electric eels lick the wet wild sea

She's a rake
with her rosebudded bosom
Laughter
pirouetting before this frozen sky
Startled birds tumble from my shoulder
Words collide with low-flying clouds
Blinking cursor shuts down

Sating my appetite
for golden calves
she rides sidesaddle
down a dirt road
me riding shotgun
down the waterfall
of my spastic dreams

With moist fingers
I tear
at her chocolate wedding cake
her whole being more
than the sum
of its crumbs

Tossing ballet slippers at rhododendron
she leads me to her secret nest
where she feeds me perfect grapes
me slurping the juice from her sliced peaches

The wheat in the farmers' fields ripple
Yellow corn bow to wind
Three strokes past midnight
the owl hoots
its velvet starlit oracle
trees bleed
as thrashing blue-eyed sailors
swallow salt
shattering on rocks
she practices
her two-step
on

I close both eyes
plunge in

A virgin
in spiked heels
she pliés above the silly stones
and laughingly displays
her lavender bandaid
earned bending
love's backbone

I collide
into colors I feel
The mountain shrugs
Knowledge fragments
and crows plant rain along
the roots of chaos.

•••

She does not walk
  on water
 she treads in babbling brooks
    the white dove flutter of her skirt
    the pirate swagger of her hips
  her toes outstretched
   slicing paths
    through laughing rapids

She glides
  down waterfalls
   angered
   if her hair gets wet
  scolding the solemn pines
   the willows weeping
    the forest fickle
    with stupid stones
   and pungent death

When she crooks
  her index
my feet I forget
 as I slip and slide
  across the corners
  of her smile
clutching the invisible rope
  she does not know
 she tosses me

I savor each brush with her lips
      swallow her verbs
      caress her nouns
      question her adjectives
as separately
we dance toward
      engulfing sea, she with
trepidation but without fear
me riding the humpback whale
of a deathwish
      the loss of life on unearthed land
      the loss of dry eyes
the loss of a rippleless existence
      safe inside my carapace
the pearls of oysters
forever out of reach

Her sails hoisted
      thumb to the wind
her fingertips waltzing
      the brown of my arched back
      as I bask
      in the reflection
of her honey-soaked skin
while stars
      disguised as liquid
      descend the mountain
        bright-eyed
          and gigglin'

She does not
      walk
    on water –
      but I do.

•••

Morse code comes like morning sickness
Gooey chunks of last night's resolve
Steamy stew of mixed metaphors
Signifying love   at its half life

Words are warriors, caress
a doublecross; arrows have angles
splitting the Adam's apple
yanked from my throat
dangled over my head

Sparrow   broken wing   tiger claws
search for lion who loves like lap dog
tongue is ribbon yanked from hair
color blind, slicing all tender loin
with razor-sharp suspicion;
seasoned deception built
out of sand on beaches of long ago

'Cross white picket fence
chat with Aunt Agnes
dream of Prometheus
stallioned atop you
creating a tidal wave
as he rocks you
endless
in Venus's half-shell

Back to earth, criticize
curdled milk, bruised fruit
bleached souls left in the desert
gossip/recipes/Aunt Agnes/Simon Sez
misery can be made almost pleasant

Living in fear of bottom line
Fear of distant train
Fear of child, mud on her shoes
Fearing truth might prove to be true
Living in fear of varicose veins

Call, then shun, then coo, then curse
then caress, then kill. . .
Afterward, pick up your jacks
All remains quiet along the cul-de-sac

Save the contentious snores
of Aunt Agnes which bores
your gargoyle heart
into rearing again
its existential head

When the nude mice of your latest experiment
are too frazzled, too defeated to trip
the lever of yesterday's cheese. . .

When a choir of clouds appear 'cross eyelashes
rattling the table of contents
in your Ozzie & Harriet Earhart dreams. . .

When your broken treaties somersault
to sprain their knees on
the floors of dime store manikins. . .

Once again you will skim
the Book of Ruth
while tanning under a sun
that bares its teeth

Once again you will jaywalk into my arms
forge your driver's license

spray paint the cathedral
sigh into my synapses
even as your buttered knife
prepares to make its first incision

In sickness and ill-health
till deathness
do us part – she was kind
to dumb animals
      it was the smart ones
      that gave her problems.

• • •

I moan for you, Lisa. I moan

Your sweet breeze brushed a lonely ocean
Those lips tripped my shins
I savor your smile
      even as soaring gulls fade dim

Would but those distant eyes
        those stars with a woman's gaze
      those candles aflame in your lighthouse door
    would but they did perceive
        the vast weathered ocean
   begging solace upon such soft-skirted shores

Would you heard the roar
        of these waters
    or breathed the brine that time
      has kissed into sensuous thunder
   and reins like Apollo his sun:
      firm hands in deft command

at each wink
of his gold-wrought mind

Whatever man lies beached in your bosom
I share his sigh
Whatever dreams give purpose to our pillows
Whatever waters fill the bottomlessness of each
our naked lives
We can but abide the tide
to the sun our shaded eyes
to the moon our faded glow

And so I turn
as I have often turned
one tear this soiled cheek down burns
my sobbing sails fixed on that sagging blue horizon
An Achilles in rags, an Icarus falling
A Ulysses outwitted by bankers, brokers
and Aphrodite

I moan for you, Lisa. I moan.

LOTUS EATERS

It waddles to the podium
boasting of its arrest
for stalking a bottle
of liquid sex

Tobacco stained
corn row baby teeth –
          eyes blinded
     by naked clarity,
          jowls masticate
to the swill & swell
of an abandoned masterpiece

He laughs w/the wild-eyed
two-step of a homeless
crazy person
          as he upchucks
the moon thru his sieve

The distant embers of a campfire cackle, cough & hiccup

Fearless before gods
it is the Goddess
          who wrestles him
to his pigeon-toed feet
          car crash & fender-bending
          oceans surge over a bedrock of simile –
while a middle-aged clock
ticks & tocks
          reminding the murky mirror in the riverbed
          that nothing is more tragic
than a death
that continues to live.

•••

We once walked together, this brother and I
Walked for miles in silence that understood, that said all
We walked while others laughed and loved
Our hearts humble, our faces stoic
We walked till the gods embraced us,
Severed us from our past, then from each other....

My other now grows bitter, lost in a drunkard's blindness
Imprisoned in a mask he mistakes for his visage
And like a wounded animal, prepared to devour even the hand
Of the brother come to nurse him

A bend in the wind whispers: sail on
Forget this brittle & broken bottle
There will come others, already
New arises from ashes grown cold
Worry not of him but beware the Antinous
For he knows not what he does
And with conscience clear
May one day slit your throat

Fear not the heart's throes
The aches & arrows of love unsavored
Let your sister rend your heart
Let sweet pain soothe you like a breeze
For like a breeze, so too your sister returns

All this whispers the wend in the wind
Echoed by seagull, hawk & heron
A phalanx of clouds storm the horizon
While gray-haired mountains ruminate
And tottering pines remember.

•••

The wonder of rouge
That can blacken blue scars
So the unsuspecting world can slumber
In innocence

What power in the powder
That can deny the screams
The flailing arms, the angry heartbeats
Of violent love turned frustration

So you take the morning off
Consult your druggist
You dab before the mirror
A make-up artist
With your paints and postures

You enter the office at noon
And turn your head askew
Everyone looks but none see
And so the bitter night
Fades into blackened memory
To haunt you only
On the howl of the next full moon.

•••

Blemishes parade in their Easter Sunday best
        So infinitesimally small, they dominate the big picture
                Turning words into sirens & silence into conspiracy
Their bibs are stained with mustard of their own making
        Their drool trickling to shoe where it coagulates

Becoming a sticky goo they blame on you & me
But they wear hats & pay taxes
Condescend to marry blemishes less perfect than themselves
They rock on squeaky stools while criticizing crickets
Complain when wind is zero degrees too far to the right
Or when left isn't left enough. . .isn't left behind. . .
Isn't left alone. . .or isn't just plain left

They shop at convenience stores where opinions
Have that soft, pliable texture of silly putty
And new niggers can be manufactured
Before old ones are quite used up
Syphilitic Zorros, they piss their john hancock
Setting jars of Clearasil aflame
On lawns of anyone honest enough to be themselves

At high noon the inflamed epidermis patrol
The pockmarked face of Lilliput
Littering the streets in their finest
As old maids wave white hankies
And politicians loosen their belt

Who was it who said:
"God is nothing more than that crack in your mirror"?

● ● ●

My parents made me do it
I was not a serial killer at birth

When I was five
Peeling scorched skin from screaming redheads
        was the furthest thing on my mind
Till my parents made me eat beets

My father   hobbling thru life in broken English
My mother   maternal angel of "Woe is me"
          nagging us into doing everything
          her way   every Sunday
     we had to sit & listen to Lawrence Welk
Do you have any idea   what all those bubbles
          can do   to impressionable youth?

My parents drove me here
          drove me here to torture you
They all but gave me the car keys
          practically held the steering wheel
My father: a well-intentioned man
          but the other kids all laughed at him
I   had to bear a shame
          he was too stupid to even see
Why couldn't he be like other men?
     Why couldn't my mom
          be like the moms on television?
                         –they never wore curlers
Did you ever see a hairnet on Mrs. Cleaver?
Did you ever see Timmy's mom
                 in rolled down stockings?
I   was a sensitive child
Made in God's image   my innocence all-knowing
Till they drug me thru their swamp
          chained me to inadequacy
Fed me dysfunctional dinners
          meal after meal of mediocrity –
     they were the ones   who led me down this dark path
          this psycho path   that sends me howling
Every time
There's nothing to watch on tv.

I thumb thru the tv listings
     same o sitcoms   cop shows
       repeats from the 50's
Gunsmoke   Bonanza   Lawrence Welk
    Lawrence Welk   Lawrence Welk
  and oh, oh...
Bubbles start foaming from my mouth
     I get this urge to do something creative
     with a corn cob
All because when I was nine
My parents made me eat the whole thing.

So scream   curse   writhe   die
Yet understand
    it's not my fault
  understand
    it's not my fault
behind these wild eyes   this jagged giggle
     this blood-stained smile
deep   deep   deep   deep   really way deep down inside

    I'm a pretty nice guy.

SONGS OF THE SIRENS

It was a hot fudge Sunday
    the day Wednesday's child
    fell for girl friday

It was Tuesday that
    he held her hand
    as a plump ripe cherry
    split in the western
    horizon, crimson juices trickling
    onto whipped cream clouds

On Thursday she sighed into
    his synapses, sweat pouring from her
    forehead while a forgotten sprinkling
    of stars dripped across a blueberry
    sky & the moon, shaped like a cashew,
    melted as she moaned to her gods

On Saturday as he was soft slipping
    into sleep, her body sweet &
    thick like butterscotch,
    their tongues heavy from
    each other's syrup,
    she whispered: *I love you*

Then it was a hot fudge sundae
        all over again.

●●●

She wanted a lo-cal reality
She wanted a God she could press
                    between the covers of a book
She wanted peace without preservatives
            a president who saved whales
                    who changed diapers
            who got all the capitalists to acknowledge their greed
She wanted a lo-cal reality

She wanted no cholesterol in her Christmas
                    no fat on her Thanksgiving turkey
She said we could force feed the ignorant
            educate the hungry
                    with diagrams on how to chew
            and neon signs reminding them to eat slowly
                    paid for by capitalists who
                            finally made to see the light
            would donate immediately to atone for their greed
She wanted a lo-cal reality

And she did not want to be filthy rich
            Just have enough to buy the things she needed:
            a larger wardrobe, a bigger apartment with French
            doors, sliding windows; a car with sun roof, CD player
            A/C – and maybe have a little stashed away
            so she could quit her job and travel
No, she did not want to be filthy rich
Just have enough to never have to worry about money
                            and never have to cook

She wanted her men to be biodegradable

The kind that mowed lawns, raked leaves
Took out the garbage before being asked
                              lowered toilet seats

She wanted death eliminated in her lifetime
She said a low sodium polyunsaturated jesus
                    would appear on an orthopedic cloud
                         zap everyone evil
              along with viruses, papercuts, unfaithful lovers
                                   and mosquitoes

She said *he* would have the foolproof diet
              he would not cast out whipped cream
                    pistachio nuts, maraschino cherries or
                                        chocolate syrup
Divine love alone would keep her thighs thin
As she sucked on the bones of paradise, gobbled its fruits
              guzzled wines more succulent than the sum
              of Man's earthly sins

She wanted a lo-cal reality.

● ● ●

The house that bought John
              looks like any other
John beams when he shows her
              It's his first:
He, one of countless many.

The house bought John on a rainy
              day in May. The first of May.
Mom & dad & friends

gathered for the signing of the contract.
Brother took pictures.

The house is now in need of repairs
  The door sticks
  The eaves drop
  The windows stair and pine
John works in the basement of the house
  that owns him. He saws & drills
  & rivets. At night he satisfies
  her beams but by daybreak
  Phoebus like a peeping tom
  pokes his yellow finger thru every gaping crack
John slaves tho he knows the roof won't hold the snow.

● ● ●

So it's a beautiful morning
Pimple sun   screaming yellow
 scurrying squirrels
     oozy jello green
Sky bleeds bluer than Coltrane

Love cuts like a fast food hamburger
   I told her
Our hearts sat down to tea
 lips quivered rat-a-tat-tat
   rapid pistol fire
  eyes dropped bombs
    fingertips dug trenches
She said I was shitting Tootsie Rolls
  that the wrappers had unwound
That wolves would swallow the moon

                                    which is why
                    the moon pays wolves no mind

She who had split pyramids
        whose soul I had seen undress
                whose every whim presented a resumé
                        who once said to me
God is a barber
            snipping our locks
                        while he confabulates
            with best friend Jesús
Old man Jesús
            crosslegged in the corner
            chewing lower lip
                    flipping thru *Field & Stream*

I believed in Presidents
Doing little else than delivering mail
She
    wanted them to hose down
Sidewalks. Love cuts like an orange
        she vomited up to me
While I summoned St. George,
                    the dragonkiller
The secret to happiness,
                            I said
Is loving yourself
Over and over and over

Love cuts like an orange
        she repeated
    to someone resembling me
*Your problem
    is you didn't use condoms*

                        With that
Her wings hailed down a taxi
Leaving me
            to settle the check
            multiply by two
            move decimal two places
20% she had taught me
                            Tea turns
To poison
When your waitress gets stiffed.

                                    ● ● ●

Love, how is one to define
you? You, the trickster
You, the chameleon. I have
seen thy dimpled face
vanish the moment I thought
I clasped thee. I have
suffered your fever when in
the other your virus did not
exist; or, after a mild cough,
could not persist. You've
come dressed as lust, a
swaying skirt in a vacant shell.
You've come as friendship,
tingling with possibilities,
but like a dream vanquished
as glare of morning fell.

And yet, without you there would
be no will, no trying – for how often
have my aspirations died

to be resurrected by a sparkle
you flashed in another's eye?
With your patron saint Hope
you weave delusions of grandeur
and for an hour a week a month
I am Superman, I am Mohammed
more than certain all mountains
shall come to me – tho none ever do.

Do you laugh on such occasions?
Or do you mourn? You who will
dangle me in the dreams of others
yet keep my heart still. You
whose foot gets tangled in the
twisted language of the wounded
ego. Or, who in more
passionate souls will soar
then explode, like a phoenix mistaken
itself for an eagle.

What is your true face
I wonder. Is it passion?
Is it faith? Is it sacrifice?
A giving that takes?
Do you last? Must you change?
Is the test to recognize
despite the doubt, the hurt
the disappointment, the straying,
the vain longing that obscures
your name?

Sometimes I ask myself,
Have I ever loved?
And I answer, *Yes.*
I remember the pain.

If I were Achilles,
My heart would be
my heel – vulnerable only
    to a woman's nail.

•••

Sea spouts jet mist
        pushing upward
                    out of rock
Sunshine suckles your milky shoulders
Volcanoes rumble
            but won't erupt – still
        the way you wear your day
                    determines the Dream's look

A bleating heart rattles 'gainst cold cage
            bold yet sunken
                    like ships whose full (moon)
        lonely lips
                    alone break
                            the undulating surface
        where   surf / salt / indecision   drift

The shadow of Venus casts a wide net
            fishermen dream of abandoning their fishes
    they rock to & fro
            the wet bottoms of their boats
                        sloshing in rhythm
        to their lack of understanding
w/not even stars to guide them –
                    just the heart beat of the naked soul

The shadow of Venus
        looms in pink puffed clouds
Persephone cleaning house, setting table
Diana weeding her tangled wilderness
        while Athena   half-listens   to lieutenants
           in heated conversation –
  rocking on her patient porch
      she resumes her reading
          now & then gazing outward
          now & then peering a thousand miles inward

When the lieutenants leave
      Ceres chimes from a full-raised window
         chairs scrape, pans rattle, voices clang
         smiles are passed from plate to plate
    each aroma a moment to be savored

Vesta lights her fire in the hearth
      while Hera, at head of her table,
hums melodiously
     as she braids the moonlight
           that bounces
    across the black inky bay
where raft-borne Odysseus stares
      at a lighted window
        & the dark-haired figure
          haloed in its homely frame.

LORD OF THE WEST

As night wears on in the village square
You can hear the sighing willows
      wending in a godless wind
You can hear the mountains wheeze
      as a lake-cooled breeze tumbling
            rushes in

As stars fade in Heaven's dim-lit shade
Dew-backed grass blades quiver
      Trees on sad memories shiver
Like that apple-selling old maid caught tender
      on a hailing homeless eve

While youth wail on white unruffled sails
You toast pale, dying cells clang limply
      'gainst the luckless lock of time
As snarling winter-white hounds, hellish bound,
      howl tales of life's most ghastly rhyme.

• • •

A locust stands alone in tall grass
Grandfather was too kind for this world
Its leaves tremble, shrivel, wither

My grandfather's brown bony fingers on broken glass bleed
The locust roots are gnarled, arthritic hands
Grandfather's smooth bald crown shined over a slanted forehead

The locust bark is pockmarked by the woodpecker's beak
His head grows weary, falls heavy to the pillow
Boughs and brambles rattle in the wind

Brittle bones give way at the hip; at day's end he is bedridden
The locust uses the sky to break its fall
Grandfather also used the sky – as the sky used him.

• • •

I rake leaves
          as Apollo peers down
          cat-pawed on twisted boughs
of mighty trees –
               in words
          that hold no sound
we talk of dying and
          this friend frozen found
                    stripped of his last breath
          his last flutter of a laugh
               cascading thru our breeze –
          a billion atoms
                    tumble into grass
               static-clinging to bent
disbelieving knees;
          friends
               dangling in the grapevine
          stutter & gasp
                    strip-search gray matter –
          while mere moments   forgotten
     surface   mellow   bloom
in the glaring yellow
                    of this fierce high noon

Petty concerns
                rear-end themselves,
        pre-occupations screech
        to a tire-squealing   halt
        as we contemplate
                the big black question mark
                on the door before us

                Tho the news was sudden
those who were with him last
believe he knew
it was coming
                which makes me wonder:
        did Death don a dark hood
        or loose flowing locks
                        beckoning w/perfumed wrists
        & scarlet lipstick?
leaving those of us
        on this other side
        to console ourselves
we hug   we tiptoe   we whisper

To avoid
        my voice
                I gather leaves in random piles
                stuff them into plastic bags
                prepare them for recycling
Apollo continues to hover among trees
        whispering my friend's name
                who whispers his
who whispers mine –
        as deafening silence
                        competes

with the scratching & clawing
of this old battered rake
as I sift thru
these mid-November leaves.

• • •

Stand naked. Strip down to raw honesty
Transcend the hidden motives, the guarded gestures
Admonish no longer that belt-whipped, scalded child
too worldly wise
to put his flayed epidermis on display
Shamed into dishonesty, frustrated into a lie
a lie that becomes a false TRUTH
that becomes you, becoming them
Be Not Them
Fence not feelings in naughts
Neither temper two-edged thoughts
To cattle or sheep preferring truth minced
in saccharin
Trust the moment and the mountain
Trust the mountain and its moment
Cast a suspicious eye on fawning excuses
on failure not fought, on fires unfueled

Stand naked to the wind, shower in the rain
Trusting what stands within
to storm what thunders without
Bare the blonde your breast
Boast Beelzebub your soul
Your wounds hail before your enemies
French kiss your fears, make love
in the stone gray temple of your woe

Stand at war with the self that is no self
      but goes blindly tripping on stones
      heel and toe were meant to dance on
Growl at those internal lies
      that paralyze your sword
      its steel pulse limply pumping
Peel from your skin that tarnished armor
Stand naked. Stare the mirror down
Let that silver-lined two-dimensional image know
      just which is real and which
      is thin shattering glass
Stand naked. The Reaper stands naked with you.

A GATHERING OF SHADES

Sometimes up is underground
On a subterranean verandah; new sound
Percolating new language; half mantra, half howl
When iambic pentameter has reached its limit
And a bloody continent eclipses the spastic sky
Where the sun wears false eyelashes
And every dandelion becomes a critic
When Humpty Dumpty is tumblin' down
Sometimes up is underground

So when the heart's voltage assumes fetal position
And the flies in your mustard crack a wan smile
Consult the long-haired spiders chewing cobwebs
Dance with roaches, chat with Frankenstein
Don't let that cat in your tree fade with a frown
Get your soggy soul down under
'Cause sometimes up is underground.

● ● ●

I keep hearing these voices
Like horses stampeding the steppes of Asia
Voices from the pregnant shadows
Pounding on drums & in rivers
Tapdance echoing down hollow halls of routine
Voices that as soon as you hear them
They're gone

Now I know these voices
Are *just* voices, with no consciousness

A funny twist of wind
Distorted refrigerator hum
Pipes knocking on my subconscious
Yet the message in these bottles is so distinctly human
    Sure the words are nonsense
        a few muffled syllables scribbled in air
      vanished when I jolt to attention
        when I squint to see the ink
    on pages already passed
But it is not the words, it is the voices
    clear, close, human – it is the voices

Voices in the rattle of venetian blinds
    in the sound of women scraping their knees
      as they search the floor for the precipice
    in the softshoe of penguins sashaying down main street
    in the jackhammer of skinheads spitting watermelon seeds
I hear voices of scarred children who sigh like weeds

I hear voices in the sneeze (God Bless You) of the widowed spider
    in the bloated implosion of potato men
      who douse their pain with kerosene
    as cameras click there's this southern drawl
      a morphined speech
I hear a cry in laughter at fall time
    violin voices quivering thru crinkled leaves
I hear voices in the swish of a sister's sleeve

The voices speak of Nero...Nerological madness
    of the anarchist who would be king
    of corporate giants swatting flies with newsprint
    of Death, that soft-spoken baritone

                    with the high falsetto scream
        of saber-toothed neighbors chain-smoking rumors
        of Kierkegaard watching football, Kant
            sending out for pizza, Lady MacBeth
                    sucking penises that turn to lollipops
            when she dreams
I hear voices in the squeal of rusty mattress springs

I keep hearing these voices
Like horses stampeding
Voices from the pregnant shadows
Voices that as soon as you hear them....they're gone.

● ● ●

Lay me down in this city of nights
Where things lost then found
            carry a *disease* all their own
Where a stark moon stalks voices w/out lungs
    below that black underbelly
                of a stiletto studded sky

Where each moment stutters
                in baptism with desire
            raucous jazz pouring onto the streets
            cigarettes once lit   left to burn
                under stars suffering from Alzheimers

Where the summer coils like a snake
    thru the broken glass of laughter
            & backrests of bus stops
                become havens for poster childs
    & lanky, wire-rimmed men
        wearing their Marxism like measles

Lay me down in the land of pacing panthers
     where death cracks its fart
  && organized dirt
       perfects the science of its sewers

Let your black holes suck me dry
   below the thousand-eyed brick mountains
Weave me in & out of traffic
   strobe lights flashing neon brilliant
      from red to green to gold

Lay yourself down in this city of nights
   recharge those sun-drenched batteries
let the wet lips of electricity's kisses
   course your dark-eyed soul
        till spastic memories calm to rest
        & scars transform to masterpieces
in the brilliant glare of Dawn's replenished son.

● ● ●

When I gaze into a melancholy sky
One blanketed in gray, the sun a dingy
Stain in a smoke-sooted ceiling, I fret
Not the frigid wind, the oblique slash of rain
The gnawing termites at my soul's bones.
Neither do I sigh as I watch sad
Rivers of traffic belch at stoplights
Or managers dangling in neckties, egos
Swaggering, or staggering teenagers
Jiving on the static of afternoon redeye.
One tear, one tear only do I spare for missiles
Saluting like soldiers, stern, resolute,
Obedient to push-button orders. "Man is

a failed crop," pimp pushing philosophers say.
Aye, we have known dry winds; even
Orchestrated our own drought. We have known
Torrents and knocked knees at thunder, and
(having manufactured thunder, bottled it and
Dropped it on ourselves) have trembled at
Our own terribleness. We have spread seed
On rock, in blood-soiled mud, along the fertile
Crescent of madmen, entrepreneurs, salespersons
And prophets. We have flooded deserts,
Smothered swamps, hammered ore into bullets,
In cauldrons mixed poisons children
Use as bubblebath. Weathering boredom's
Drizzle by fanning whims of bearded
Tyrants, we have carved our scar, etched
Our initials in history's gushing cheek; we
Have made more than Jesus weep. Yet when
I think of those who plowed this dirt before me,
Who read truth by stars, turned sand into
Windows, who made rhyme, and rhythmed,
Chiseled truths into stone, who smeared
Dyes along high arched ceilings and
Breathed soul into slaving in the hot sun
Billowy clouded songs; when I recall those
Who shivered in the lighthouse as
Winds whipped at cobwebbed windows and
Fog enveloped fast fading moonglow; what
Great ghosts haunt these halls
Ghosts named Plato, Socrates; such great ghosts
Do haunt these halls, with short names
Like Homer, Buddah, Dante; and long names
Like Michelangelo. Names noble like Napoleon,
Humble as jesus; mad as Nietzche
and Van Gogh; reverent names: Confucius
Lao Tzu, Saint Paul. And men and women who

Left no name at all; but, counseled by
Ghosts breathing in books, dancing from trumpets,
Quilted in blankets to keep warm what's young,
Have lifted boulders and turned back floods
Have parted rivers and dared the will
Of pharaohs. When I recall such ghosts,
Once flesh, once muscle blood and bone
Whose spit lit candles, whose cries
Fanned failing embers, rekindling the tearful
Triumphs that fuel the communal campfire
In the black forest of the human soul;
I realize Lincolns, Einsteins, Aristotles
Will continue to sprout among us. No cloud
ever extinguished sun; Truth
Shall forever rise from ashes of fallen angels
Earthquakes shall forever scatter empires
Mortgaged on greed, hate, lies. So let the
Thunderclouds cackle, let the mortars grumble
Let the rain rain red. Any second a deranged
Uzi might mow me down on a shopping mall
Sidewalk, another brain-splattered blade of
Grass laid senselessly dead; still, grateful I
Tumble this raging psychotic sea, bolstered by
Ghosts who once plowed this ocean before me, who
Unearthed among rocks, roots, worms and
Trees that rough cut gem called immortality.

THE CATTLE OF THE SUN

Ah Beauty, what sweet faces thou doth wear
Thy countenance of fiery trees marooned
'Mongst clouds and streams and mountains white at noon;
This autumn could not find thy face more fair,
And yet thou glow in cheeks and chins, in soft
Expressions flow from chaste and moral souls
Whose dance just like a symphony unfolds
When thy baton conducts their strides aloft.

Fair Beauty - in sight, in words, grace or sound
Thy silken skirt rustles and hearts beat time
Ears smile, eyes follow as Truth's bold rhyme
Echoes 'cross centuries hemmed in thy soft gown.
Stay Beauty, through thy pupils let me gaze
'Gainst thy bosom let lie this soul in praise.

● ● ●

T'was a most uncertain time of year
The mind of Mistress Nature not yet clear
The third craggy month, well into its march
Still, hoary handed Winter held cold watch
While budding breasts nipp'd & tickl'd the air

Young Spring's burgeoning bosom held firm against
The frosty grasp of Winter, gnarled & bent
On chilling all verdant aspiration
Till sun smiled on Winter's perspiration
And warmer winds bade the cold old man repent

Two forms did perch on yonder rocky slope
Mr Death & Madam Love with force of words did grope
To ascertain which of them might be the stronger
As if victor were he who talk'd loudest, or she who talk'd longer
Which gave Resolution scarcely a hope

"Men fear me," bawl'd Death who stroked his bristl'd beard
"Have not shrines, mausoleums in my honor appear'd
Pyramids & yards where grave stones congregate
The world doth mourn the victims Death hath ate
I must be the stronger for I the most am fear'd."

"Besides," continued Death who clear'd his scratchy throat
"My spell is permanent, once dead – that's all she wrote."
"Your spell is hardly permanent," Love fluff'd her hair & scoff'd
"What dies becomes reborn. Life rewinds its clock
Ignorance alone doth fear to don Death's cloak...

"My spell is such sweet nectar, many crave
While others run post haste, thinking to flee more brave
Still they fall, one by an other bewitch'd
The hide & seek of hearts, mind & souls a'twitch
Gladly, or sadly, they're all wrung thru my maze

"Half the world, mostly the fairer sex
Would fain give all for Love, such do I perplex
The other half tho wise or strong & handsome
Will once or twice submit – a weak-kneed Samson
Deliriously content – crippled by my hex"

But Death would not concede to Love the greater might
They argued all the day & thru the wide-eyed night
When Dawn awoke the two were at it still
The sun, warn'd by the moon, did near avoid the hill
While birds from lack of sleep took drowsy flight

When all at once Love paused, a comma in mid-phrase
A shadow, a noise, a figure roam'd the dew-dropp'd haze
It stopp'd on edge of deadly precipice
Hair slapp'd by wind; eyes tired, cold, adrift
A poet, she surmised, by his blank, moronic gaze

"Let's ask the yonder poet to resolve this matter square
Poets have sung Love's praises since days did form the years"
To ask the poet Death did readily agree
Certain Love would now, surely, finally, irrevocably, see
Poets above all else the knelling toll revere

"Fair poet," called one. "Noble sir," the other said.
"A word or two," they croon'd. "Give us pause, let known your head."
"Opine for us your thoughts on blissful Love."
"What think ye sir of Death, Life's darker dove?"
"What words on matters weighty can your wisdom shed?"

Our poet gazed up slowly & quickly he divin'd
The eternal struggle t'wixt these conquers of Time
Love who made mere minutes stretch eternal
And Death, condemning Time to his dark infernal
Each wishing th'other negat'd in clever rhyme

"Love is magnificent poison," the poet then began
"It puts death to Boredom, gives Purpose a helping hand
For me to live or die did once but seem the same
Till Love blew sweet kisses & whisper'd a fair-skinn'd name
Then suddenly to live was something great & grand

"Love is a rich adventure, savory, delicious
Where hearts become foolish; delusion nutritious
Not fetter'd by temporal uncertainty
We glimpse in that other our bond with infinity
Tho soon enough we feel stifl'd, possessive, suspicious

"But Death, Death is a lover too
The kindest of lovers, tho Love & Life think him cruel
Where Love fades, Death's firm grip holds on
Where Love hurts, in Death all pain is gone
The illusions of Love in illusive Death stay true

But what be Love without Doom or Doom devoid of Love?"
Here the poet raised his brow, then scann'd the clouds above
Hearing naught a peep from Love or Death
He sigh'd, took a deep breath
Envying the flight of yonder unquestioning doves

"What is Love without fear Death might erase it?"
He ventured on; "Where be Love if Dark Doom could not encase it?
True Love must now & then become reborn
The old must die, that a new Love love on
'Tis Love's sweet duel with Death that leads us to embrace it

And Death, where be your majesty if Love could touch no man?
'Tis loss of Love & being loved, gives weight to your harsh hand
Otherwise Here or Gone 'twould be the same,
'Tis our loss of loved ones that be your horrific gain
Why else fear we to nestle below your sand?"

With that the poet stood & bow'd his head
With running leap ov'r the edge his nimble figure sped
But as toward bottom his body came
He whisper'd, then shout'd, a female name
Thus Love & Death in his final act were wed

Now Mr Death & Madam Love both shook their puzzl'd heads
Believing not a single word the clever poet said
Yet as they left, they did admit
This one sure could spew the shit;
And make it rhyme: he must have been well-read.

●●●

The three-ring tent unfurls its flags
The tiny man is watered down
Chimpanzees parade in pinstripe
While elephants exalt the clown
High heenas laugh at hobos
Humming bottle busted blues
Scarlet-ribboned vixens
Pass practiced pigeon coos –
It's springtime at the circus
On Colfax Avenue

Thin men donning bracelets
And tigers stripped of stripes
Prance, prod, prank down Broadway
Sucking metallic pipes
McDonald scores 3 zillion
Acrobats line in queues
March in uniform grease stains
And cud the second-hand news
It's springtime for the circus
On Colfax Avenue

Staggers Ringmaster Nose-Red
Down castles of cracked concrete
Black panther strokes the bearded lady
Ringmaster, Jr. sniffs his feet
Roaring comes lion tamer
Maimed his MOM tattoo
Hunts the polluted half-mooned night
For a face to nail his screw
It's summertime at the circus
On Colfax Avenue

Travel east, see Kitty's pussies
Travel north where colors race
The slanty-eyed, the thick-lipped gentiles
The Spanish slur-named slum their case
Their numbers bulge, their eyes swell red
Their young in bathrooms sniff taboos
Delta queens and cocaine kings
Prosperity's residue
As summer slips through autumn
Down Colfax Avenue

Take a turn on Residence
Where green of trees and grass
Out glow the naked concrete
Where casual strollers pass
A bird chirps to his sweetheart
They share a wormy stew
The sparrow, the squirrel, the blackbird
Mix with human brew
And ponder: Why this monument?
This Colfax Avenue

Children caked in mud pies
Young eyes that shimmer like silk
Adults hone their hobbies
Taking suckle on talent's milk
Then someone bakes a smile
Defrosting a song or two
Jugglers dance on unicycle
Laughter peels the hues
As if to say man is made from child
And never an avenue

Matthew rocks to sidewalk shivers
And rolls towards new wave band

Douglas recites crisp poetry
Rhythms from the Motherland
Jan and Ann stretch and pull
To earn their dancer's due
While Barbara spins the wheel of fortune
Molding praise from the potter's pew –
Praise to the struggle forgotten or lost
Along Colfax Avenue

Neil flutes from infancy to fancy
Skywise, he floats in paints
Sweet Lilly with voice of six, nay, seven angels
Turns to Buddha and bids him be her saint
Mark, his pen is sheathed, it's silent
A comma gives pause to pointed tool
Lady and baby need bottle and brick
And dreamers more practical tools
While Mike with pencil sharp and poised
Careers down Colfax Avenue

Somewhere south of main street
Basking on sandy beach
On the isle of good intentions
Docks the anchorless art reach
With burning bush extinguished
New captain and new crew
Set their sails for sunrise
Their rudders for souls of rue
In the prisons, in the droolhouses
And down Colfax Avenue.

● ● ●

a lump of coal crushed
to form a diamond:
a crystallized
inverted
tear

—black—
and white
study in
negatives

granite cheeks
forged from steel
steel eyes
steel wool
steal away
to a dark room

double exposed
she slips
out of foc u s

Cockroaches
scurry   down
cobbled streets;
photographs
line   bullet-
ridden   walls:

h o l l o w -
c h e e k e d
fish   mongers;
feral   cats
in gu t t e d
- h o m e s -

the   war-torn   crooked   fences;
broken   bones   of   refugees   with
backs bent & furrowed faces, they
hobble past, averting their eyes
to   avoid   the   lopsided   enemy

Eyes black as
the coal in her
christmas stocking,
lens splattered with mud
she pans – grown
men mill; mope
beguiled

as she mines for the
glimmer & sparkle
btwn missing teeth
of a cautious smile

Rice farmer
runs   thin
fingers thru
thinner hair

Diamond eyes   snaps a photo
a moment   is stolen
& for one   click of
a second all   sad ness
t u r n s   g o l d e n

●●●

A slender woman in the wings waits
                    call her: EXPECTATION
Her petals unfolding,
        her perfume, her butterfly flutter
  are late
    yet the blooming in my brain
                    submits to the tease of her brother
                        call him: FATE

The crowd mills   sufficiently warned
as the hurry of the instruments
        clutters a space filled by silence
that snakes into sound: the pound
the pummel of stretched skin
        the deep, throaty bass
        the voice in the microphone
hovers, then
hunkers home
        while guitars   syncopate

The slender woman rattles her bracelets
        sisters chomp their gum
        servants & guests
tap their toes in rapt attentiveness
            to the lackadaisy
            of her brother's a-mused strum

Prickly flowers raise their stems, tilt their heads
        sway to the melody

until the clock again (as it always
        does) strikes midnight &
        someone writes w/regretful pen

                              a skinny check
while a glass slipper
                falls thru a crack
        in the stairwell.

ONE MORE STRANGE ISLAND

Somewhere btwn mud and heaven, this forgetting
this never-knowing the known, this denying
what like bone permeates our imperviousness to We

Somewhere btwn dirt and stratosphere the right
to take away what cannot be taken except
on pain of inflicting pain which always returns
to haunt, to hang somewhere btwn rock and ruin

Somewhere btwn flesh that walks and the firefly's
bright remark – cocktail in one hand, cigarette
in the ashtray – comes (almost always arrives)
the red cries of conflict's burnt meat

the boil on the battlefield, the orator on the scaffold,
the noose that despite the wisdom of talk shows
fails to discriminate btwn the Notary
and public stamp of Good & certifiable "Evil"

Somewhere btwn the idiots savant
and the sycophant idioci is the remembering
that only remembers to forget.

● ● ●

They have declared war, these towers that rise above you; they have
hot-wired your car, tapped your phone; targeted children and ignorant
bystanders – for terrorizing ignorance is their only means of getting at
you.

They orange your waters, turn bloody your air; disguise themselves as
telephone poles, spitting electric death rays up your spinal chord in
hopes of striking a sympathetic vibration.

Can they be satisfied?
Crushed into submission?
Placated with better television?

These towers have hearts of chiseled stone, eyes of tinted glass;
backbone of US-grade mining disaster steel. Their elevators have
gone on strike; revolving doors are revolting; restrooms are for paying
customers only – even the janitor's mop is poised and loaded.

You had best use the emergency exit. It's gonna be a long lonely
limousine ride now that the caviar is radioactive; now that the sniper
has changed his tune; now that the ideals with which you have skinned
the natives have rolled on their bellies, cocked their pistons and aimed
their angry gods at you.

● ● ●

Wild Flowers in a forest of sorties
My bride comes to me in low skirt and veil
Our fathers barter with goats, sheep and missiles
While I wonder: how thick her ankles? How
raven-like her hair? The goat-footed nomad blows
his hollow hornpipe while holy men wallow under
shade of troubled trees. A Scud whistles by like
an imam come to wed us. I wonder, come the night,
if a Patriot will stiffen and rise to the occasion
My mother hums the tune of the Tigris River

and consoles me with tales of her wedding night
How fear, apprehension turned to pain, to blood,
to bliss. How acceptance dulled her sorrow
and love for her children made tolerable a tyrant
With Allah, she said, there is always collateral
damage. There were surgical strikes long before
there were B-52's. Still vain dreams of youth
muse of Love's sanctuary: in a bride of morning
smiles, in a wife as moist as pomegranate juice
Will we barefoot through the desert, where worms
follow and eye us? Where the stained glass of
history makes red the shame-faced moon? Will
our children have their wrists tied with yellow
ribbons while the hooks of democracy reel in
fascist loaves & fishes to be divided equally
among the starving multitude?
Wild flowers in a forest of sorties
My bride comes to me in low skirt and veil
Our fathers barter with goats, sheep and missiles
While I ponder: how thick her ankles
How raven-like her hair.

● ● ●

"In history, even the lies are true....."
Lucille Clifton

Dear Osama,
 Sitting Bull, Geronimo & Red Cloud greet you;
 we have heard about the travesty and read
 with great sympathy your complaint.....
  but be advised: in history, the lies are true

Mirror, mirror on the wall
Who's the fairest of them all?
            Snow White...with her seven dwarves.
            We too were once terrorists
                        scourge to civilization
                        threat to their freedom –
        like your Palestinian
removed
            from the land of our ancestors
                as if our rights,
                        our desperation,
                our starving   and slaughtered children
                        did not exist.
He holds these truths to be self-evident:
that all men (except those in his way) are equal.
        Like you, we evaded their cavalry
        attacked instead white picket fences
        and SUV's parked in two-door garages
                where our teepees used to be.....
                        while out in the yard
                                their broken treaties
                                        flapped in the wind
and for that we were the barbarians;
            made to crawl on our wounded knees
                wrapped in blankets of small pox
                        herded like our buffalo to near extinction.....
        and so we feel compelled to warn you, Osama,
that in history, even the lies are true

Mirror, mirror on the wall
Who's the fairest of them all?
    armed with Manifest Destiny & his Good Neighbor Policy
      spreading good will and good Cheer – that

              n e w   improved
              laundry detergent
              ●GUARANTEED●
              to take the dinge
              out of indigenous
              ●GUARANTEED●
              to white wash
              any dictator's
              bloody   j e a n s

        – by the way, Osama, Che Guevara sends his greetings;
He holds these truths to be self-evident:
    the death of a million Indians
    or a billion Arabs
can never measure up to the comfy lives
    of even just a few cozy all-consuming Americans
        and you, Osama, you slew more than 3000...that makes
you EVIL
    & all her bombs,
        incursions
            subterfuge
                pre-emptive strikes
                    waterboardings
                      & assassinations
                          "Good"
Mirror, mirror on the wall....
    Perhaps you thought in lashing back you
    might reveal to her her sin....but
        Snow White has slept with a 1000 dogs
    and still remains a virgin – read her history books

Mirror, mirror on the wall
Who's the fairest of them all,
>   Snow White, pure as the driven snow
>   her children playing cowboys & indians
>   pure as the driven snow
she will bury you in, Osama,
because in his-story even the lies are true.

ISLE OF OGYGIA

Gulls screech out
    a seven year nest
    a tender isle
        of gentle sensual supple caress
sultry gales, soft giggles
    seashore a welcoming dress

I sing with pen
Pound with drum
Recite to mortal gods
    imprisoned in my own wake

The rocky reef reckons
    scylla & charybdis beckon
 I hold my course, chart my escape
            with stars my only friends

Her sweet rum cake
her finger pudding, Queen Circe
      grows an old maid
her patient breasts   ebb and flow
knowing all too well
        a man's a man
    and a sailor's a landlubber exiled by Fate
    his thunder throbbing, aching to plunge head first
                in wet slimy coral

Abandon this voyage I would not
    Penelope waits
    And Telemachus must a father
      to teach him to fish, to fight & to father

But this vessel's near worn to raft
    the crew cares not for commandments
    the head needs an open pillow
        tears need lips to dab & dry them

And lo! a half-goddess who will oil my limbs
        as I stare out at Poseidon
        & contemplate the hazardous last legs
                of this Sisyphus journey.

● ● ●

Sit back   Relax   Feel the day
Feel its up and down
        white ocean waves of circumstance
                we can't control – only put our stamp upon
Hang on tight
        for that rollercoaster ride
            the tunnels of love
            the houses of horror
            the hall of mirrors reflecting
        only our foolish selves back   at our foolish selves
Clutch at straws: anything's better than drowning
Sooner or later
        you'll make it back to solid sand
        and up the rollercoaster again
                bumping your skull on stars   so high
                you think you'll never come down
But you do...you always do... the lake stagnates
                and the mosquitoes send you on
So sit back   F e e l the day
Feel the sun's knuckles kneading your back

Feel the harsh frost: winter's womanslap
        putting red in your cheeks
                and that fiery dance to your breath
Feel the prickle of mowed grass under unhurried feet
                          R e l a x
There will be time to DO
        to mount your charging steed
                to rescue feigning damsels in distress
                        to suffer the dragon's ingratitude
But for now
        admire the serious silliness of kittens on the prowl
        note the architectural wonder
                          of towering storm clouds
        stare into the billion eyes of midnight
                caress the velvet air
        tap your toe to the reggae of crickets
        synchronize your clock to your heartbeat
                your breathing to the rhythm of the sun
        there's something to be gained
                watching that ant drag a potato chip
                          across the lawn
So sit back   Relax   Feel the day.

● ● ●

AFLOAT. . . .on a small shifting planet. . . .sifting sentiently thru the
dark snake of time. . . .dripping revolutions. . . .rolling to the rhythm, the
rock'n'rolling bebop boogie and jive of whatever comes down. . . .Afloat
. . . .an unfinished rambling tapestry in a mosaic of time. . . .War is but a
fart with a putrid long lasting odor. . . .a martyr's death is an anal fixation
during an oedipal moon written in the stars and edited for television. .
. .still we scratch spit and backbite to play leading man, to waltz with

leading lady – want my autograph? . . .that one throws up her neurotic nose as she tries to save her marriage. . . .one last time, again. . . .that one: numb in the womb of his booze and his bacon, preparing his belly for by-pass operations. . . .and they: peter pans with a bone to pick: consumers, congesters. . . .condemned to labor for laborious sake. . . .always forgetting: we are but dust afloat. . . .on dust, afloat. . . surrounded by dust afloat. . . .in time, afloat. . . .afloat. . . .a banana float has like purpose. . . .ah, but we've something a banana float has not – choice.

Ay, we are the choosing animal. . . .afloat, and yet steadfast in our resolve to give form, to give reason, to give purpose to the darkness. . . .A sneeze! . . .And yet, a dignified sneeze. . . .proud and quarrelsome. . . .in a hurry to remain where fleeting memory imagines we have been. . . .And so the exoduses, the crusades, the genocide, the lawsuits, the news cameras, the brides, the babies, the bombs. . . .the hurry hurry hurry for fear heaven may up the rent, or hell foreclose on our houses. . . .Time will never run low. . . .but you will. . . .and I will. . . .we will trickle thru the ourglass. . . forever churning our new beginnings toward the same ol' endings. . . .forever. . . .forever afloat. . . . senselessly. . . .sensuously. . . sometimes serenely. . . .But always choosing. . . .forever dissertating that this choice be the more rational. . . .the more real. . . .the more realizing than the others. . . .Happy in the unhappy struggle. . . .and demented by that day of leisure. . . .the day there be nothing to do, but float. . . .float. . . . .climb in the swimming pool and float. . . .stoke up the hot tub and float . . . .lay down the sword, the hammer, the ledger. . . .light up the pipe, lean back. . . .and float. . . . .

● ● ●

Like sand through the hour glass so are the days of our lives
Like sand so are the days through the hourglass, our lives
Like sand our lives thrown thru the hour glass
The our glass of our lives so is the daze
Like sand are the days, hour lives
Thru the ourglass, through
Hour daze like sand
So are the
Lives
Our lives
Through THEE hourglass
The ocean's silence; pounding roar
Looking through, toppling onto the sand
That is hour lives; the stops, the false starts
That make long our daze through the hour like glass
Sans the beach where gulls soak pigeoned feet & waves foam
On their breaker journey home to the sans of our glass lives, thru the daze

Like sand throw the hourglass, throw too the daze of hour lives
The heartbeat's moon-drawn ocean, hour-thrown thru the glass
Of desire's dreams onto wet sand for gulls to nibble, for gods
To negotiate, for ocean's slip to soak with seaweed
Throw the days like sand upon the hour
Reflect like glass the lives
Sifted as sand
Upon Thee
Hour
Sans rhyme
The ocean's rugged
Rhythm beating ragged time
Through each hour, so too the days: hour
Lives of sand shaped into glass; dazed, contorted
Reflecting sun and harboring the prints of gulls whose lives
Seen thru our glass renew our vast ocean, make reason of seaweed &
Like sand through the hourglass, so too renew the days of our lives.

THE SANDS OF ITHACA

She was like God to me. A huge woman
With breasts the size of cows
And arms as wide as trees
The hair on her arms bristled like pine needles
She smelled of lilacs and evergreen
And when she giggled, laughter in bubbles
Foamed from her mouth as natural
As trout tumbling in a fresh water stream
She was like God to me

I would sit for hours on her pregnant belly
And gaze into eyes at once blue
And gray and brown and green
I would hike upon her mountainous bosom
Roll down her soft brown flesh
Make snowmen from her dandruff
And find myself where I had been not lost—
only hidden
She was God and Mary and Jesus to me

And now she lay in a hospital bed
Propped up on pillows while tubes like tentacles
Pierced her blotched, bruised flesh; her eyes puffed
And cut where hours before they bled
They had dragged her to an alley
These ants who call themselves men
Whose priests genuflect to books and deeds that read:
She belongs to them, to do with whatsoever they please

So they nibbled at her flesh, gnawed
The back of her neck, drilled for her blood
To run their machines; till they flattened her breasts

And then fought wars over the right
To devour what little was left

      Yet she who was like God to me
Smiled, even though to smile was to strain
And she reached to pluck the tear from my cheek
For it was not her fate, but mine, she feared
She, who is God to me.

                    ● ● ●

The dentists are at work aside the Union Square,
Pounding, scraping, drilling the grey metal teeth of progress;
Thick, callous hands never rest
Even in the clinging fog of dubious mornings where
Pedestrians scurry across the cold damp concrete and
Dull traffic horns blare in the incessant distance below;
Even as hot steam pours from the city's jaws
The dentist works – drilling holes, filling cavities,
Building crowns and root canals; his deft hands
Gently maneuvering his resolute tool:
The fat chapped fingers of dungareed steel-eyed man

The maple doesn't care with what bravado the wind blows
The man straightens his tie, smoothes his hair
The oak will not die for refusing the vote
Nor does he fear the man with the veto
The elm knows also bone's ache, brain's free fall
The man splashes his face, slicks on deodorant
The willow bends to touch its toes as
The man catches the bus that coughs as its doors close
Exhaust lands on the maple, the oak, the elm, the man
                    and the willows. . . .

• • •

Awash, ashore, wet brown Ithacan sand caked,
flaking from salt-bleached sunburnt skin;
chest heaving sighs for Poseidon appeased;
seaweed strapped about bruised, wobbling knees;
slap of brine-scented foamy sea
slashing blistered travel-tested feet;

blood-purple Phoebus melts the morning mist,
owl-eyed, composed, serene; uncloaking
simmering sky-sermoned sea;
flaming hoofbeat of chariot steeds
atop white-splashing gull-crying waves
of moon-deserted day. Ulysses

stirs, stumbles, sits; clutching seaweeded knees as
the briny siren-echoing breeze makes
slaves of his god-tossled salt-studded braids;
nostrils quivering, memory aflame;
the woodlands whisper: Artemis,
supple limbs, fragrant airs, leave-rustling peace

meadowed in laureled hair – a saline tear
our algaed hero weeps, shipwrecked by uncertainty
badgered by one-eyed men, his raft
on rocks reduced to splinters in his feet.
You aren't home yet brave cunning Ulysses;

your weathered body won't know calm sleep till
bow is bent, till arrow proves true;
for how besides is your Hera-eyed Penelope
to know you? Go, talk with the
hoary-headed herder of swine and the

wisdom-woven stranger trodding down yonder
parched dust trail; gain that goddess's
sympathetic ear for the face you bear
is not the face your widowed wife looks to,
is not the face her dreams wear. Ulysses,

adrift tho ashore: a beggar, bristling beard,
dank dark rags to shroud his homecome shoulders
his shipwrecked lifemate wedded to his wave,
yet doubting the harbor of his mirror gaze;
cautious with her kindness, eyes straight forward,

while her heart evades; as rude
suitors parade her feasting hall, savor
her wine, await her strict measure;
they congregate, they salivate, urinate as they
postulate the fate of his treasure.

Crouched in a corner, aged Ulysses
must wait as broadchested Apollo
steadies his steeds toward dusk's darker reefs;
and Aphrodite closes her knee
to brash young lieutenants, with their scented locks
and their lotus-coated pleas.

•••

I was there. . .when God was born,
I was in the delivery room
I heard Him holler when the devil slapped His face
mistaking it for His Holy butt.

I bit my nails as this overweight nurse with zits
& a bad hair day wrapped Him in a blanket,
wiping the slime from His shriveled face
cooing, and assuring us everything was cop-a-sect-ic.

I was rocking on my front porch the day they brought Him home,
home to grace our neighborhood. . .suffered
His terrible twos & those tantrums that destroyed
whole cities & razed the walls of Jericho.

I was pacing the pitcher's mound
when He tried out for little league
insisting we let Him bat clean-up. . .and we did
because nobody wanted to piss Him off.

And we held our breath when He hit puberty,
impregnating virgins left & right
blaming it on His Holy Spirit.

And it was me who said "Say cheese"
the day I snapped the photo for His driver's license: He
legally allowed to ram his front fender
into Hindus & heathens.

I squirmed in the bleachers as He & His frat buddies
belched during homecoming,
divine puke gleaming in the bushes
their visiting Pilgrims slaughtering
our Indians, 1776 to nothing.

And I remember the wedding. . .the cake. . .the circles
around the bride's eyes – hell, I even babysat
the self-righteous brats who call themselves His children.

And I saw Him fitted for His three-piece suit
the one He bought after changing
His mind and deciding the root to all evil
wasn't love of money but lack of it –
that. . .& homosexuality.

Yeah, I was there when ol' Yahweh was born.
I guess you could call me a Yahweh Witness.
So you can take it from me; cause I can tell you first hand:
His mother....
                had the miscarriage.

FEAST IN THE GREAT HALL

First you take a boy
Maybe dye his skin, say brown
Shake well in a pot of hopelessness
Turn his innocence upside down

Sprinkle in lots of let downs
Peel away the self-esteem
Grind up Mom too tired to care
Blend in Dad, drunk & mean

Grill with friends till medium rare
Season with coke or pot
Or sauté in the frying pan of poverty
Till he's longing for what you've got
And you know what you've got?
You've got a recipe for death

Add a pinch of envy: like a boastful cousin
Greased & garnished, talking jive
Cruising down easy street, laughing
Heaven on earth – if you survive

Bake these ingredients in polluted air
Simmer to the point of boiling
Pay no heed to any cries for attention
Whip & burn till this boy is broiling

Mix him up till the world's against him
Melt his dreams in impossible knots
Till the only joy in life is the quick fix
Till refuge & home is a parking lot
And you know what you've got?
You've got a recipe for death

Reduce & roast, scramble & steam
Let him stew till the time is ripe
Meanwhile dice & strain any love for others
Till there's no regard for human life

Now comes the most important ingredient
Flambé this boy into a man
First marinate in a neighborhood gang
Then stuff a gun in his angry hand

Stir up some foolish hero
Who puts the boy to the fatal test
Who dares the boy put up or shut up
And takes a bullet in the chest
And congratulations
You have successfully completed
Your recipe for death.

● ● ●

Jesse, you had it all wrong
Busting thru vaults w/six gun ablazing
        – a waste of good bullets
Instead of bandana   you should have wore a tie

A briefcase would have made a better holster
          combination lock   instamatic smile
          with cufflinks to match, Jesse
                              you could have gone far

Instead of contraband goods in some abandoned mining shack
          & whiffing the farts of the Younger brothers
You could have been eating your neighbors, chomping on busboys
          pouring your gravy on a thick thigh-of-peasant
          & doling out prostitutes as christmas presents

You could have played musical chairs w/vice
          presidents, generalissimos, gunrunning colonels,
          and those mafio sol a mia's, not to mention the
          ambassadors to those swiss family bank accounts
          Robbing-son Cruise-so, here we cum.....but no, Jesse
You refused to read the book
          The one they faxed to you
          Along w/that credit card application

I'm telling you Jesse, you had it all wrong
You don't need spurs – just a Masters in Manipulation
Hell, I hear it even comes with a gold-plated
                              matching pen & pencil set
Then you could have paid someone else to take the chances
                    paid someone else to wield the gun
And as you well damn know, Jesse
It never hurts to be born a president's son.

● ● ●

This little piggy went to market
This little piggy stayed home
This little piggy had roast beef
This little piggy had none
And this little piggy cried
"Wee, wee, wee," all the way home

This little piggy sells at market
This little piggy sells his soul
This little piggy chops a rainforest
And that little piggy rents the hole
And these little piggies cried
"We, we, we," all the way home

This little piggy played the market
This little piggy sold drugs
This little piggy had an army
And this little piggy sold the slugs
While the unarmed little piggies cried
"Wee, wee, wee," all the way home

This little piggy drove a dump truck
This little piggy used a phone
That little piggy made a fortune
But the other little piggy got none
So that little piggy cried
"Wee, wee, wee," all the way home

This little piggy climbed the ladder
So this little piggy bought a home
But when this little piggy got laid off

This little piggy had none
So this little piggy cried
"Chapter 13," all the way home

This little piggy owns the market
This little piggy owns your home
This little piggy invests your savings
But you, you little piggy, you get none
All around the world little piggies are crying
"We, wee, wee," all the way home

This little piggy is your President
This little piggy is his son
When these little piggies go to trial
These little piggies get none
So these little piggies cry
"Hee, hee, hee," all the way home.

● ● ●

You yourself have said it: power corrupts
Yet when that gilded bride was offered thee
Thou didst clasp her like a whore between thy teeth
Thou didst boldly burping take up that cup;
While untangling the mangled chessboard
of genocidal stench, star-spangled
Didst thou stoop, raise arms, set table and supped
As if thou hadn't heard: Absolute power absolutely corrupts

They dub thee Superpower, vulnerable only
To dwarfs, and cash registers that flatter
Nibblin' on sautéed leg of peasant, charbroiled,
Served on silver platter; for the price of bananas

thou dons bandanas of darkness
Dressing paranoia in a white ivory tower,
Wallowing in a bay of pigs while smoking joints
With mafia hitmen; meanwhile thou turns
Thy head from the cry of swollen babies
Preferring instead the bloated bellies of uniformed
Brown-nosers snorting coke while preaching pepsi

And all the while you sunbathe in the background
Toting democracy, your golden calf icon...
               ....and then you scratch your head
When mobs spit at your news cameras in places like Iran

You yourself have said it: Power corrupts
—& masturbation makes you blind.

● ● ●

Rome   now   has a president;
               they say he's a god
     out of a burning bush
comes George – George I-can-not-tell-a-lie
               Washington, King George,
Saint George...the dragon slayer
     for what dragons there are to slay!

George raises his sword
               when you pull the right string
pull another string and he lifts his head,
          smiles his crooked smile
and proclaims:
     "The only good injun...is a dead injun!"
proclaims:
     "Why our niggers is happy.

They love slaving their lives away.
Why, without us they'd still be running
in the jungle...naked."
proclaims:
"Those sissy fags ain't datin' my sister!
Sure I believe in equal protection
under the law, but
that ain't human:
I'm human. In fact...I'm a god."

Rome now has a President
the best president money can buy
Cocksure the cock in his hand
is anyone's but his own.
Cock-a-doodle do
as blood mixed with oil spews
(baby seals flap their flippers
gasp for breath as he takes a bow)
Cock-a-doodle do
as he twists his screw
into anyone who refuses to be just like him.

Rome now has a President
they say he's a god
his blown-dried hair
waving in the breeze like amber waves
of grain; I pledge allegiance
to his flag   and to the flagging of his justice,
his "Just Us"; no matter
what that reconstituted constitution says.
"Ahem! The problem with the poor is they starve too much.
Take away their food...that'll teach 'em!"

Rome now has a President
compassionate...conservative....

so conservative you barely see the sleight of hand
as empires collide   and tyrants rise
        to become U.S. certified champions of democracy
        while keeping their own people under
lock & key   and away from the American press.....

So conservative you barely see the sleight of hand
as you balloon to three times your normal weight
        (But hey, it's good for the economy)

So conservative you barely see his lips move
to say: "Alright, yeah...we did topple your democratically elected
        government & slipped in our puppet who tortured-slash-killed
        tens of thousands of (yawn) you people. So
        what's the big deal? – hey, look! it's almost time for lunch...
                think I'll order veal."

So conservative you barely see the sleight-of-hand
as freedom fighters are "poof!"
        transformed to terrorists
the moment they aim the weapons we sold them
        back at us.

Rome now has a President
                    they say he's a god,
            a compassionate god
        who cares about his people
            and only his people
(heaven help you
            if you're not one of his people)
Have you ever felt the wrath of God?
Just
        keep being different –
                        you will.

PENELOPE

What purpose there be?
But be each a rose – each seedling to blossom
  each smooth petal to glow, till crippled we
    crumble and to moist mother
      earth we go

So why the struggle?
You, and me, and those about us who stumble, who,
  like we, chisel and hoe to plant in this garden
    from stone that bleeds blood –
      a perfect soul

Upon thy green stem
A red rich sensuous rose; a confident wonder,
  gentle as doe; tall, alert, erect,
    sentences strong, heartbeat of
      clear, concise prose

I could not love you more
And yet, you suppose a love with claws; scissors to clip
  in bride's trousseau such elegant thorns
    to grace some watered vase
      atop some bureau

What purpose for me
In loving this rose? Why water with kisses?
  Love's light why bestow? Why, but to watch a woman glow
    that the world know her scent
      and her scent a nose.

• • •

We stand equal height, seeing eye to eye
My brooding orbs tread light grazing sweet yours
To look & delight into that sparkling core
Those pupil-pierced worlds I know not of –
Yet know I know. I know I know

Those rockets of gray like shooting stars
Amongst the soft brown earth of thy heavenward hair;
That heart, also of the earth, a tender plod of land
Trampled upon – raked, hoed, plowed and fallowed;
I know but one rain and lonely glisten of dewdrop

To give so slender a flower so nobly gentle a form;
That grace is more than grace from God
That innocent elegance with which your every
Limb, smile, touch, playful saunter, every look
Askance does natural as air possess;

Such elegance was chiseled onto that smooth wise brow –
You calculate, proceed with caution
You fear to tread on limbs that shake in wind
You fear the fall thru empty air, the sun you fear
No mortal man you trust...and I, alas, am mortal.

● ● ●

      We speak in tongues, you & I
tongues   intertwined thru the slime
               of so many lifetimes;
    from the slippery of the snake
          thru Noah's doubt-drenched tide
you have slithered, I have slathered
     you have bent like a bare-boughed tree
         and I have bowed

                    to the rhythm of your rhyme;
                                        thru suicide on the galley
the pin, the pine, the pane of plantation's crime
                    I have scorched my knees
then stretched my lizard
                            in the hot of your palm
        soaked in our sweat   trembling   straining
                to penetrate the amazon btwn your divine
btwn the ooh & the ahh; btwn the oh, yes & the oh – my – God

Once, on the bandied banks of the Nile, beguiled
                these young tongues writhed
                            our toes tickled in gurgling slime;
                                            clucking our tongues
                at the lazy wink of the sated crocodile
I roared with the cheetah
                you howled of mad ape in heat
                pressed my Prometheus btwn your pyramid
as the stone startled silent Sphinx
                    cocked its stoic brow;
my tall & dense wrapped in your thicket
                            we wrestled like spiders; mommy & daddy
            long legs lashing   in the mossy jade
    the hot muddy cool   the misty dappled shade,
                    thrashing our symphony
            among the quivering green – dashing the doubt
you harbored even then
                that I might quit this tongue's resolve
                        to crawl forever your Kilimanjaro
to climb   even thru time to
                    that wet emerald amazon
                                    btwn your diamond divine

Even now
        among bricked banks & burrowed minds
                in this cloaked & dagger time
you whisper   you willow   your wisdom weeping;
        knock-kneed & bent
        by an underground that rail rode
thru jaw of jim   thru caw of crow
        that did strip our hips of their slow mount
that spurt into shudder;
that would dampen the red coals
           of your warm welcoming stove
        to the clanging rhythmic stroke of my steel shovel

And so   humbled   we start slow
        you nuzzle the low tones on my saxophone
           my boa constricted
the moist lick of my serpent
            scaling the riffs of your guttural moans
        as you dissolve into honey & molasses
the slick of your pink
            unfolding its petal like a fern;
I savor your almonds & chocolate
        as you nibble & slurp
        my quivering thighs
           melting as you swallow my pulp
        my cornbread still probing
        for one last dip in those hominy grits
we spasm   in unison
        then curl into a pretzel
as once again our tongues intertwine
        our souls pirouette thru yet
              another lifetime;
Btwn the roil of life's ocean
        & the arresting of death's tide
        no matter the scars on the life-line

doubt you never the indeed of this will
   to scour the depths for that sweet jungle
   to close ne'er an eye till this head
     be cradled snuggly
     btwn those dark royal thighs
btwn your ooh & your ahh
btwn your oh, yes & your Oh, yes – my God.

• • •

I am the pacific, its roar, its rumble
Sometimes hushed, sometimes anxious for the beach to tumble
To claw sand, tan feet suppliant, breakers humble
To bubble like an idiot, for sense into passion crumble
I am the pacific

I am Beethoven's 9th symphony, joy strained through sorrow
A storm stirred to rain, replenish rivers, flow into tomorrow
My kettle drums in crashing waves Man's breath to borrow
To sway his soul, universal undulating unity in tow
I am the 9th symphony

I am the All though one alone – a constellation
Pressed into a star, a shining tear in recitation
Within the Grecian ocean chorus, a choral invitation
For melody to rise and flow in swilling restoration
Of the One in all

Yet I am clash of salt, I burn with whirling vanity
Both a reflective lake and trickle of sanctioned insanity
The slap at shored rock, the lichen on stony beached humanity
I am the clash

In me the crash of foam, a bitten canine
Charging the pack, jowls white with twirling whine
I jump, I crash, wet back supine
I am the crash

The crash of pacific ocean, the clash of pacific ocean
The hush of stars, of symphonies, sorrows strained
The slap, the foam, the bitten canine
Kettle drums in passion waves, whirling, a bubbling idiot
Clawing sand, a storm of rain, in Grecian chorus
Twirling in suppliant breakers to joy's slashing
Pacific waves

I am the pacific, I roar, I rumble
I bubble like an idiot, to your supple breakers humble
Sometimes hushed, sometimes anxious for your weave I rush, I stumble
Foaming, rolling, waving, craving your sense into passion crumble
Into my pacific

You, me: a 10th symphony; wind's violins we'll borrow
Our kettle drums like cresting waves sustained beyond taut strands of
sorrow
Two throbbing breaths, two panting breasts rushing toward
tomorrows
Gliding on the swelling strings, weaving melodies from bows
That know the symphony

You, me, the All in one – humanity in restoration
Our tears shining; two stars astride the constellation
Two voices, one chorus, one chord, one soul in recitation
In harmony to rise and roll, our cymbals crash in invitation
To flow with One and All

But oh the whirling crash, the salt of vanity
The reflective trickle, doubts, fears, insipid sanity
The slap, the sting of pebbled beached humanity
Oh, the crash

And oh the twirling slash, the whimpering whine
The mad white pack of drooling canine
Charging to beached destruction, in sense supine
Oh, the slash

The slash of pacific, the crash of pacific
Two stars astride the drooling doubting pacific
The hush of waves, whimpering crests
'Gainst passions weaving, 'gainst throbs and swills
And kettle drum breasts; the taut strands of joyous sorrow
As fear into melody heaving, foams atop crashing
Symphonic waves

Into the pacific ocean, its soar, its tumble
Your supple breakers round my knees in sand supine we stumble
To babble like idiots, before humanity humble
Rocking, heaving, foaming, rolling from crest to restful crumble
Into the pacific's symphonic ocean.

TEST OF THE BOW

Oh St. George, what have you done?
You have slain the dragon
Burned its carcass in the sun
You have hacked its limbs
Its belly axed into 20 parts
But oh, St. George
You left intact its heart

Though you've slit its wrists
Gouged its eyes, shred its tongue
Snapped its head off with a twist
Though scale by green and wicked scale
You have sliced the beast apart
Oh, St. George
You have left intact its heart

Listen: hear its hoof beats, its hammers
Its iron wheels, its cattle cars roar
Feel the pulse of its trembling temples
Listen to the thump thump of children crying
As they crawl across an ethnically-cleansed floor

Oh St George, put down that gong
The beast you buried yesterday
Is putting galoshes on
Waist-deep in red rivers
You feed its fledging crop
Oh, St. George,
This dragon is a clever fox

Its claws now nuclear iron
Its teeth of stainless steel

Its mating call the screeching siren
While grave stones shake their heads with disgust
Oh, St George
Can we ever slay the dragon that is us?

• • •

Triangle Man
floating among the stars
on what planet will you alight?
Who among us could receive your
                              sharp edges?
Who could gaze into those pyramid eyes
            without squaring his jaw
            or circling her wagons?

Isosceles on the Mount
          with a hypotenuse around your neck
mumbling parables only parallelograms
          understand. That is your legacy
                    Triangle Man

You with your wrecked angles
          must float forever among stars
who themselves once had jagged angles
till they found their corner in the universe
and caught afire.

• • •

Lay your ear close, you can hear it breathe
Hear it? – It's that low monotone hum tuned
To your heart thump; feel the rhythm of its stillness –
Cause and effect tumbling into silver-white blood streams;
Bubbling volcanic pus, red as a blemish, red as war,
Spewing life, limbs, and death which feeds life
Across its moon-circled petrified skin –
Climb its spine, that hard-humped vertebrae
Of time-humbled dinosaur, pockmarked by abandoned anthills
Where once antennaed Helens gazed upon opposing poles at war;
Run naked through its photosynthesizing beard
Smell the pine, the eucalyptus, the sweat-pearled green
As morning like a brisk-breezed ocean
Tumbles through its everbristling hair –
Combed by us: Adams orbiting history,
Membranes peering down tubes at one-celled constellations,
Geometric combinations of wind wrapped in earth,
Of water breathing fire, of need want desire:
Respiration – Aspiration – Expiration
Corpuscles pumped pulled dragged kicking
Down paved arteries, slaves to cells, lost nuclei
Vital organs in the mass reproduction of riveted trees
And pigeon-dunged cities; our road maps patterned
After palms of apes and aspen leaves;
Prisms found in oily wings of flies
Yellow rivers igniting lamps so God's blood-veined eyes
Can study power's pathogens, antibodies
Cancer and crime as we mine gold rivers
From cavernous walls and watch red rivers split Adams
To short-circuit the central nervous system of All –
Put your ear closer, feel its pulse thumping
Like tires to wet road, like humans humping
Like time tapped on typewriters, like frogs in a forest
Like impetuous wind at rest, like a preacher in prayer
Like the slow squeeze of tyranny, the soft sweep of despair

Like an ocean's hushed brine-tossed orgasmic moan
Like the munching march of termites
Like the slow slow s l o w r u s h h o u r home
Like wind through dry leaves is this speck of dust
This earth, this atom that breathes.

• • •

The snake has shed its skin
The apple given way to gravity
With the serene blush of indian summer
soul and season are a tapestry of colors
A virgin has delivered him
on a seashell

See the moon's gold shimmering halo
The jealous God has released him
The waters parted
The mountain ceased resistance

You will know him by the minotaur
that is his shadow
Against his breast, the shield of Achilles
in hand the bow of Ulysses
which bends like a willow
at his mere caress

And before him
the Buddah, Mohammed and Jesus
scatter rose pedals
marking the path that shall be his ascent
After 40 years in the wilderness
the snake has shed its skin
the apple given way to gravity.

WARRIORS, FAREWELL

A fly
walks
across my cellar
      floor

A big
fly
with silver
transparent wings
        that
dovetail
from its black
      pill-shaped
      body
in a perfect symmetrical
V.

      Its legs
are as
thick
and black
as eyelashes –
      big feet perhaps
by fly
standards.

      It does
not move
when I bend
      to swat it. When
I reach
to squash it

                it does
not fly
away.

                It
hasn't the
strength
                to save
itself, its
three day
                existence
nearly
spent.

A
warrior walks
across
my cellar
floor
                and
wishing her
well, I walk
                another
                way.

● ● ●

In the beginning was not the word
In the beginning the universe was wordless
Earth, wind, molten motion
Gurgling incestuously; a wordless communion
Man created the word
That he might have a competitive edge over the chimpanzee
That he might subdue, have dominion over Nature

Even named God that he have dominion over that, too
Man created the word to separate himself
From all things, including himself
When he looked about and saw
What he had done, he saw that it was no good
So he created a word for that, too.

2

Candle burns above coffin of flesh.
The language of rain. The cloud's cough.
A broken bridge. A dog-earred longing.
Gargoyles perched atop withering dreams.
It is said she met with the back of his hand
It is said he met with the begging of wind
Side by side on their pillow of darkness
He kicks the tires. She stirs the pudding.
Concrete meets the snake's coil of affection.
Time becomes something we must trudge through
When did walls change to ceilings?
Who removed the love from grandmother's soup?
When did I forget to heed the whisper of leaves
Or that a blade of grass is a kindred spirit?
The glow worm above stutters in a hurricane
While skeletons of zebras glisten, brittle as fine china
Scattered in a bullring.

3

    In the end words shall be wordless
Presents we exchange at Christmas
Thoughts wrapped in ribbons
We strip away to get at essence

In the end we will value our regrets
As fertilizer to our successes
We will know again what we have always known
        In the end a spiraling staircase
Will be lowered, our half-lives lifted
Clouds will tiptoe past the shrapnel
Of other people's opinions
        In the end holding hands will be
Like clasping stars, trees will
Wait for our breezes, robins will
Steal our laughter and
Mimic it in their songs
        In the end the children that sleep
In our bloodstream will rise and stretch
Each limb a universe only love could spawn
        In the end we shall all stand wordless.

● ● ●

He walked...he walked in January
when grounds were frozen...he walked where wind wore teeth,
its tartared overbite pressed against his window pane,
icicles drip   drip   d r i p   d r i p p i ng   silver muffled screams

He walked when hurricanes blew young
when bees sang & birds with melodies stung
he walked thru buzz & babel, teetering as earth quaked
marching to the heart beat of each different ache

He walked where skies were blue, eyes bluer,
souls bluer still; where tornadoes scribbled with fine point
cursive letters of Hope divided by Disappointment
then multiplied by zero. *And you can't divide by zero,*
his teachers said. You can't...but the world could

He walked when hurricanes were full blown, when flowers
touted their full regalia & words like roses wilted a day
or two after spreading legs full bloom. He walked
where Love & Hate were college professors shaking
their rulers, gazing over bi-focaled lenses

He walked where blinding beaches singed
his toes as the sun rode him bareback
& the moon pressed down his heavy wet shoulders

He walked up ponderous hills, down existential
mountains where leaves exploded & trees fell
in forests unnoticed & philosophers disbelieved

He walked, him & Hunger, singing "God Bless America"
off-key; knocking door to door on Halloween
dressed in his compromises, opening wide
a bag of barely recognizable dreams

He walked scraping his knuckles, tossing bits
of his flesh at cackling geese; he walked till the gods
of Pro & Con lay fat & lazy...tho unappeased

As he walked the Thanksgiving turkey
sifting thru potatoes, carrots & peas for the
gobble gobble gobble that would make okay
what by any other name would still be sung
"My Country 'tis of Greed"; he walked till
Wall Street fell the last Christmas tree...

And still he walked...dragging his feet,
casket heaved on one shoulder, flicking his butt
at a white-haired priest as he leaned on a shovel
patiently waiting while the gravedigger took a pee

And he walked as stars fell like snowflakes, galaxies
melted like ice cream, God's long tongue licking his face,
he walked till nothingness became his first,
his last & middle name. And still. . .he walked. . .

up and down that split second called eternity
he moon-walked, & stubbing his toe on the Big Bang
somersaulted, landing once again on her infinite feet

pausing only long enough to tie a shoelace
she gobblety-gooped her way into another
screaming, squirming birthday suit

checking her compass, smearing on mascara,
make-up & sunscreen as she continued her walk
across the four walls of the sky's limitless face
slipping on sidewalks of stars & rain

as she struggled to remember to not forget
to remember something half-vaguely forgotten,
something teetering the edge of her nervous restlessness,
just beyond her spiritual reach

something about an infinite universe
         (in finite space
something about an infinite universe
         (alive with death & decay
something about an infinite universe
         (God a schizophrenic you never outwit
something about an infinite universe
         (with all the comforts of Dante's inferno
         & never never ever a permanent place to sit.

● ● ●

As lonely as a cloud; as silent as sand;
As constant as an ocean tide,
    taunt, tumbling; grumbling at gravity
    rumbling like wind to the swish, whish, swish of
              the beach-bound sea.

Meek as a mountain;
    cragged, jagged; beard of bristling evergreen
    stiff upper lipped, crusted snow cracking
    stone-cold crevices
             into aching memories.

Passive as a lake; scarred by sailboats,
    blue against a sky massive and free;
    diamonded by sunlight; streaked by the moon with
             ne'er a complaint.

Fickle as forest; a symphony of heartbeats;
    leaves whistling; bugs buzzing; the hum of
    evening's harmony; of cricket, bird, and frog;
    the rap-tap-tapping of furry mammals on the nuts
             and cones of a plentiful forest floor.

Precious as a pebble beached in oblivion;
    glistening best where no eye can see; one
    of billions of star-like stones slapped by sea,
    scorched by sun, scoured by time.

Rapid as river; no two seconds the same;
    a trickle,
        a stream,
            an angry hissing snake,
                crashing over

                              falls,
                    tripping into tributaries,
                        rippling into rivulets,
        staggering...   stagnating...   a brook...
                 a stream...   a swamp...   a trickle.

All things are a melody sung unto all other things;
The wind carries the song sung unto it
That the treetops might add the treble
The seasons its soprano, the cynic its snare
The bullfrog its baritone; the ants
Transpose the song into miniature key
To be crooned among crustaceans
To be imitated by circling bird, buzzard and bee
Who translate for the moon, stars and clouds.

A leaf falls; its echo reverberates
For all time: it too was once a cloud, an ocean,
A tide; once a mountain, a lake, a forest;
Once a pebble, a river, a snake; as it was once,
So shall it be again. The song
Remains the same – only the soloists change.

●

photo by Kit Hedman

ABOUT THE AUTHOR

One of Colorado's best known performance poets, SETH has collaborated with countless musicians, poets, actors, dancers and other performance artists in a never-ending quest to render poetry more entertaining, and thus more accessible, to general audiences. Over the years he has garnered several awards for his pioneering efforts to meld spoken word with the other performance art forms.

As a member of Open Rangers, SETH produced and directed a series of Poetry Theater productions combining poetry with music, theater and dance. He was a member of the critically-acclaimed performance art trio Jafrika, recognized by the Rocky Mountain News as "among Denver's finest cultural offerings." His experimental short stories have appeared in numerous literary publications. SETH has been a member of Denver's National Poetry Slam Team and currently performs with Art Compost & the Word Mechanics.

Discover more about SETH at www.WagingArt.com.

FRONT COVER

"Odysseus" is one of the hallmark pieces
that comprise *The Folks on Coffee Hill* suite
by the quietly masterful artist/serigrapher
Rein Whitt-Pritchette.